Dedication

The two pieces that follow were written as requirements to obtain a higher level of education. They were, I would like to think, a prerequisite of my journey to a deeper and more meaningful relationship with my Creator. During my reading and research on these projects, I fell in love with Jesus all over again. He shared insight as to how much He loves us and how special we are to Him. He has given me a mandate to share what He gave me to anyone who has forgotten who they are and who HE is.

We are never too old to pursue greater, but we have to fight the seen as well as the unseen. So. I am sharing some of the tools of warfare as given to me.

I close by saying to the Body of Christ, that we are more than meets the eye. We are the only living thing in the Earth realm created in God's image. Of all the beautiful and breathtaking images imaginable, we are and will forever be "God's Greatest Miracle".

Acknowledgments

To my Lord and Savior, Jesus the Christ, I give all praise, honor, and glory. Thank you for the words you place in my spirit to share.

To my parents, Samuel and Grace, I say thank you for believing in me and encouraging me to want better and strive to be better.

I have had the privilege to be mentored and supported on this tedious journey by so many amazing people.

To all my college professors who saw something in me and required more than I was used to giving—thank you.

I celebrate my pastor of old, Rev. Dr. Jennie Benson Vaughn, who exhibited power from on high that drew me closer to a living God. And to my pastor of today, Bishop Belita McMurry Fite, who imparts wisdom and knowledge through teaching and expounding on the Word of God.

To my family, friends, and loved ones who stand with me and by me through it all – I love you and thank you for supporting me.

Praise be to God!

God Bless You
Elder Dr. Sonoma
Suggs

DOUBLE DOUBLE

Spiritual Warfare: What the Enemy Does Not Want You to Know

by Sonoma Carney Suggs

Man: God's Greatest Miracle

by Dr. Sonoma Carney Suggs, PhD

Author's Corner, Raleigh, North Carolina

First Edition April 2022

ISBN: 978-0-9817551-2-0

Library of Congress Control Number: 2022904768

Printed in the United States of America on acid-free paper.

Cover design and typography by Hugh Daniel, Author's Corner

Published by Author's Corner, Raleigh, NC

Additional copies may be obtained either through directly contacting the author or by visiting the Author's Corner website:

https://Authors-Corner.net

Contents

Spiritual Warfare: What the Enemy Does Not Want You to Know

Man: God's Greatest Miracle

Spiritual Warfare: What the Enemy Does Not Want You to Know

By Sonoma Carney Suggs

A thesis paper submitted in partial fulfillment of the requirements for the degree of Doctorate of Ministry

United Theological Seminary
April 2011

Introduction

Spiritual warfare may be a term seldom used among some saints of God. Nevertheless, it has vastly become more prevalent day by day. There are many blood bought born again Christians who do a doubletake when asked are they waging war in the heavenlies.

The sixth Chapter of Ephesians is a very familiar passage of scripture which gives a mandate to daily clothe ourselves in our fighting attire. It then goes on to tell you why we wrestle not against flesh and blood. Okay! So what do we fight against if not flesh and blood? The only other alternative is spiritual enemies. Enemies that are beyond our carnal insight are lurking about us all day, every day of our lives. Many children of God are oblivious to their existence and presence.

As the Word proclaims to watch as well as pray, one may ask what are we watching for? If we are truly the children of God we profess to be, then he who hated God also hates us. Therefore, every time the enemy attacks one of God's own, it indirectly attacks God.

Jesus gave up His life on Golgotha Hill because of God's love for His children. It was at that time Satan was stripped of his victory over mankind. However, Satan still remains ruler over the Earth realm. This means that he still has the authority and the propensity to torment us daily.

It is not up to God to fight our battles especially when He has equipped us for every fight to come. Ignorance does not exempt you from Satan's devices. It merely makes you easy prey.

Chapter I: Spiritual Warfare

Definition

Just what is spiritual warfare? In order to proceed into the deep secrets of God and to be effective on the journey, this question must be addressed. "For though we live in the world, we do not wage war as the world does. The weapons we fight with are not the weapons of the world. On the contrary, they have divine power to demolish strongholds."[1]

Paul is telling the people that things are not always as they appear to be. War is prevalent somewhere at any given time. There are many unseen battles that go undetected daily in the lives of the saints of God.

Whether the fight breaks out in the flesh or heavenly places is not the issue. The main concern is to know that something is happening that needs to be dealt with accordingly. The words of Jesus declare, "And ye shall hear of wars and rumors of wars; see that ye be not troubled: for all these things shall come to pass, but the

---

[1] 2 Cor. 10:3-4 NIV, *The Comparative Study Parallel Bible Presenting NIV. NASS. AMP. KJV*, 1984

end is not yet."[2]

Jesus is basically saying that trouble is coming but to not be upset or scared.

Warfare is imminent. However, He has already prepared a way of escape. As in the earlier chapters in the Book of Zechariah, the people of God had succumbed to the wiles of the enemy. The angel of the Lord was sent with a "word" from God for restoration. However, one thing was made absolutely clear through those words. "Then he answered and spake unto me, saying, This is the word of the Lord unto Zerubbabel, saying, Not by might, nor by power, but by my spirit, saith the Lord of hosts."[3] The only way the war could be won against their enemies and their sinful flesh was through the Spirit of God.

---

[2] Matt. 24:6, *Holy Bible KJV*, 984

[3] Zech. 4:6, *Holy Bible KJV*, 1984

Why Is There Spiritual Warfare?

Since the Garden of Eden which scripture records, "And the serpent said unto the woman, Ye shall not surely die."[4] There has always been some opposing force against God and the things of God bringing this question to mind. Of all the animals created why did only the serpent have a voice to communicate with Adam and Eve? Why did the serpent not harass the other animals instead? How did the serpent know what God had said to the people and why did he care? These questions may never be completely answered because the Bible does not say.

This is what the Bible declares, "So God created man in his own image, in the image of God created he them. And God blessed them, and God said unto them, Be fruitful, and multiply, and replenish the earth, and subdue it."[5] The favor of the Lord rested upon them. They were given dominion to rule and reign over the Earth.

It was not until they actually disobeyed God by eating from the tree of knowledge that mankind fell. Even then, the enemy was a tempter The serpent was used to plant a seed of doubt and distention in the mind of Eve. As far back as creation, the deceiver was lurking to destroy the things of God. Not only did he manipulate the people but

---

[4] Gen. 3:4, *Holy Bible KJV*, 1984

[5] Gen. 1:27 -28, *Holy Bible KJV*, 1984

the serpent, too. "The scriptures plainly teach that in the purely spiritual realm there were angels which kept not their beginning or first estate. Thus there was a fall in the spiritual realm prior to that in the human race. There was among the angels a tempter who lead them astray."[6]

There has to be spiritual warfare because the flesh cannot wage war effectively against spirits and wickedness in high places. However, the flesh can submit to the Holy Spirit which can solicit spiritual back-up.

---

[6] Wiley, H. Orton, S.T.D. & Culbertson, Paul T., Ph.D., *Introduction to Christian Theology.* 1946, 165

What Does Spiritual Warfare Have to Do with Me?

"In creation, man was so constituted that he was a creature dependent upon his Creator, and consequently a servant of God. Yet, in the physical realm, man was the highest of all creatures, and therefore he was the lord of creation."[7]

God had esteemed man in the highest. With much love, He painstakingly scooped man from the dust. Into a lifeless form, God Almighty blew into that flesh and blood, His essence. From creation, man was the only living thing made into the image of God. "Thus when man fell, he ceased to be the servant of God, and became the servant of Satan."[8]

The spiritual battle started in the Garden of Eden and it has always been about man. The beloved of God, the apple of His eye is the object of the battle between good and evil. Though Satan will never win against God, he can take the object of his affection and turn it against him. Perhaps the first prophecy which was spoken in the Garden of Eden is the motivator of the enemy's wrath.

---

[7] Wiley, H. Orton, S.T.D. & Culbertson, Paul T., Ph.D., *Introduction to Christian Theology*, 1946, 166

[8] Wiley, H. Orton, S.T.D. & Culbertson, Paul T., Ph.D., *Introduction to Christian Theology*, 1946 167

"And the Lord God said unto the serpent, Because thou hast done this, thou art cursed above all cattle, and above every beast of the field; upon thy belly shalt thou go, and dust shalt thou eat all the days of thy life: And I will put enmity between thee and the woman, and between thy seed and her seed; it shall bruise thy head, and thou shalt bruise his heel."[9]

Jesus has already paid the cost for the redemption of man on the cross. His love for mankind is incomprehensible. That's the good news. The adversary does not celebrate the good news and thus stays at odds with the saints of God.

---

[9] Gen. 3:14-15, *Holy Bible KJV*, 1984

Rules of Engagement: Spiritual Protocol

In order to be victorious in any battle, it is absolutely imperative to have knowledge of the opponent and the rules. Being a worthy opponent is not enough. Jesus was before the creation. "In the beginning was the Word, and the Word was with God and the Word was God."[10] However, when Jesus came to Earth, He was governed by the same rules and regulations that govern all of mankind. It did not matter that He had written the rules.

"And the Lord said, Simon, Simon behold, Satan hath desired to have you, that he may sift you as wheat; But I have prayed for thee, that thy faith fail not: And when thou art converted, strengthen thy brethren."[11] Looking at this passage of scripture closure evokes questions. Jesus has all power and authority over heaven and earth. So why does he tell Peter, Satan's plan? Jesus could have rebuked Satan causing him to flee. However, He tells Peter I'm praying that your faith holds out because I really want you to make it so you can help others.

Satan is known, among other things as the Prince of Darkness. Anything in the saints of God that does not line

---

[10] John 1:1, *Holy Bible KJV*, 1984

[11] Luke 22:31-32 KJV, *The Comparative Study Parallel Bible Presenting NIV, NASS, AMP, KJV*, 1984

up with God's Word falls into his domain. Thus, giving him authority over it. God has equipped the saints and will not fight all the battles encountered, especially when disobedience and sin enters.

Furthermore, because of spiritual protocol, different enemies require different tactics. "For we wrestle not against flesh and blood, but against the rulers of the darkness of this world, against spiritual wickedness in high places."[12] Paul clearly lists the forces separately. Do all forces succumb to the same strategies? Do all the enemies just "flee" upon resistance? How do you discern the difference between a stronghold or generational curse? Are they the same? Do these forces have a hierarchy? If so, that would imply some forces are more powerful than others.

Whether this is true or false requires a more in-depth study of scriptures. However, this fact is sure that before engaging in warfare, know the rules of engagement.

---

[12] Eph. 6:12 KJV, *The Comparative Study Parallel Bible Presenting NIV, NASB, AMP, KJV*,1984

Chapter II: The Enemy

Who Is The Enemy?

The enemy is anything and everything that would exalt itself against the knowledge of God. The enemy has many names and disguises. He has enlisted forces, both seen and unseen. His army is great. As written in Ephesians Chapter six, Paul declares, we wrestle against powers and spiritual forces of evil in heavenly places. "Behind the visible structures and institutions of society and culture, evil forces are at work using these invisible powers to enslave and bind believers, to attack them and do them harm."[13]

Sometimes your inner me becomes your enemy as stated by Bishop T.D. Jakes. As free moral agents ordained by God, you may use the authority given to make choices unbecoming a Christian. In many instances, poor choices have caused pain, suffering, tribulations, and even death in a believer's life. Thoughts of immorality may seem harmless, but when disobedience is sown a harvest of sin is inevitable. Do understand there will be consequences and repercussions attached, says Eddie Murphy.

---

[13] Erickson, Millard J., *Christian Theology* 2nd Edition, 2005, 666

Scripture declares, "Finally, brethren, whatsoever things are true, whatsoever things are honest, whatsoever things are just, whatsoever things are pure, whatsoever things are lovely, whatsoever things are of good report; if there be any virtue and if there be any praise, think on these things."[14]

Regardless of the negative force that comes before you, be it Satan, demons, flesh and blood, or your inner man, just stand! "Wherefore take unto you the whole armour of God that ye may be able to withstand in the evil day, and having done all, to stand."[15]

---

[14] Phil. 4:8, *Holy Bible KJV*, 1984

[15] Eph. 6:13, *Holy Bible KJV*, 1984

What Is Satan's Purpose?

Satan, like everything else in the universe, was created by the hand of God. "The same was in the beginning with God. All things were made by Him; and without Him was not anything made that was made."[16] After God would create, He would take a look at His great works and say that it was good. These accounts are written several times in the Book of Genesis Chapter 1. Drawing from these occurrences as penned relating to creation, somewhere on the journey even the creation of Satan was considered good by God.

Man, with his many imperfections and limitations, makes and creates for purpose. Whether for convenience, gain, or just because there is an initial plan for creating. The point being that an omniscient God creates all things for His purpose and glory. Unlike man who may create just on a whim for prestige or power not always knowing the outcome. God knows. God knows the end before the beginning. Though His creations may not always work according to His perfect will, our Father always has a plan "B".

God knew Adam would fail, thus the virgin birth of our Lord and Savior, Jesus Christ. God knew Moses would not

---

[16] John 1:23, *Holy Bible KJV*, 1984

make it to the Promised Land so comes Joshua. Saul was ineffective and disobedient as the king. Out in the pasture lay a red headed boy tending sheep that would chase after God with his whole heart.

In the mind of God, "Angels in their original estate were holy beings, endowed with freedom of will and subjected to a period of probation. They were meant to choose voluntarily the service of God and be prepared for the free service of ministering to the heirs of salvation."[17]

Satan rebelled and chose to no longer be a servant of God as he was created to be. Perhaps to him it was more appealing to be the served. "Thus when man fell he ceased to be the servant of God, and became the servant of Satan."[18]

---

[17] Wiley, H. Orton, S.T.D. & Culbertson, Paul T., Ph.D., *Introduction to Christian Theology.* 1946, 145

[18] Wiley, H. Orton, S.T.D. & Culbertson, Pau l T., Ph.D., *Introduction to Christian Theology.* 1946, 167

Why Is Satan Allowed to Exist?

God is above all and the Creator of all. He alone is able to make alive or make dead. Old and New Testament alludes to instances of people and other spiritual beings chastised by the Lord for their disobedience.

Noah and his family can attest to the wrath of God. "For yet seven days and I will cause it to rain upon the earth forty days and forty nights; and every living substance that I have made will I destroy from off the face of the earth."[19] Our Father is a loving and forgiving God, but He despises sin.

In the case of Ananias and Sapphira, it was God who struck them dead. Peter confronted Ananias and told him. He had not lied to men but to God and he fell dead. Shortly thereafter Sapphira came to Peter and lied, likewise. After Peter uncovers her deception toward the Spirit of the Lord, she too falls dead and is carried away. This account is recorded in the Book of Acts.[20]

If Satan remains among us, it is because God has need of him. Satan is known as the tempter, deceiver, liar, and so

---

[19] Gen. 7:4 KJV, *The Comparative Study Parallel Bible Presenting NIV, NASB, AMP, KJV*, 1984

[20] Acts 5:4-10 KJV, *The Comparative Study Parallel Bible Presenting NIV. NASB. AMP, KJV*, 1984

much more. However, because God represents all that is good, the presence of evil causes mankind to have to pick a side, choose his master. The Lord does not make us serve him, though this is part of the purpose for the creation of man.

Satan also plays an integral part in the end-time prophesies. The Book of Revelation refers to the final war against good and evil, light and darkness. It depicts the fall of the evil one, judgment, the second coming of Christ and so much more. So it is written so shall it be done. Jesus says this, "While I was with them in the world, I kept them in thy name; those that thou gavest me I have kept, and none of them is lost, but the son of perdition; that the scripture might be fulfilled."[21]

[21] John 17:12, *Holy Bible KJV*, 1984

By Whose Authority?

Everything in creation is sustained by the Creator. The omniscience of God, which is only one of His many attributes, is a reminder that God knows all at all times. Only the Godhead has that ability. There is no living thing, spirit or flesh, that can make this claim.

All power and authority is delegated by God. "For as the Father hath life in himself; so hath he given to the Son to have life in himself And hath given him authority to execute judgment also, because he is the Son of man."[22] Needless to say that since God is the giver of power and authority, Satan received his authority from God, as did Jesus. Think it not strange that such things are possible. Jesus proclaimed, "Behold, I give unto you power to tread on serpents and scorpions and over all the power of the enemy; and nothing shall by any means hurt you."[23]

Perhaps the most familiar account of the delegation of authority rendered to Satan is found in the Book of Job. It is noted, though Satan is a fallen angel, he still has the right and authority to show up before the Lord with other angels. "One day the angels came to present themselves

---

[22] John 5:26-27, *Holy Bible KJV*, 1984

[23] Luke 10:19, *Holy Bible KJV*, 1984

before the Lord and Satan also came with them."[24]

Prior to endowing power and authority to His created, God already knows how it will be utilized. Whether the gifts will be used for ill-gotten gain, or His glory does not matter to God. Whatever the outcome, God can handle it.

---

[24] John 1:6 NIV, *The Comparative Study Parallel Bible Presenting NIV, NASB, AMP, KJV*, 1984

Chapter III: Satan's Arsenal

Deception

Before delving into Satan's arsenal, it would be beneficial to see what Jesus says about this fallen angel. "The thief cometh not, but for to steal, kill and to destroy;"[25] It is understood that he is the prince of darkness. He has taken it upon himself to defy the Will of God. He has many titles such as, angel of light, Lucifer, deceiver, liar, tempter, adversary, and the list goes on. "Satan is not simply the personification of evil influences in the heart, for he tempted Christ, in whose heart no evil thought could ever have arisen."[26]

Though he is crafty and skilled in deception, there are only three categories by which the tempter operates.

1. The lust of the flesh
2. The lust of the eyes
3. The pride of life

"For all that is in the world, the lust of the flesh, and the

---

[25] John 10:10, *Holy Bible KJV*, 1984

[26] Vine, W.E., *Vine's Expository Dictionary of Old & New Testament Words* (John 14:30; 2 Cor. 5:21; Heb. 4:15), 1997, 992

lust of the eyes, and the pride of life is not of the Father but is of the world."[27] The enemy's desire is to bring chaos to order. He is skilled in his art and has had years of practice dating back to the Garden of Eden. "God gives light and truth; Satan tries his best to cloud light and truth with darkness and lies. His primary tool is deception, convincing human beings that the lies they believe are the truth - even the truth of God Himself."[28]

When looking at the true meaning of deception, it primarily means "to ensnare, to corrupt; especially by mingling the truths of the Word of God with false doctrines or notions and so handling it deceitfully."[29] This tool may be the most effective and deadly in Satan's bag of tricks. "If you really want to buy the lies that Satan sells, God will not stop you."[30]

---

[27] 1 John 2:16, *Holy Bible KJV*, 1984

[28] Beam, Joe, *Seeing the Unseen*, 2000, 12

[29] Vine, W.E., *Vine's Expository Dictionary of Old & New Testament Words*, 1997, 27

[30] Beam, Joe, *Seeing the Unseen*, 2000, 13

Lies

Lies and deception are very closely related because deception begins with lies. God stands for truth. "And ye shall know the truth, and the truth shall make you free."[31]

The Bible declares that all have sinned and come short of the glory of God."[32] The deceiver is so cunning that he can mask a sin within a believer then add pride and arrogance. This combination culminates the belief that one sin is lesser or greater than another. The Pharisees were skilled in this area. They looked upon others with contempt and could not acknowledge their own shortcomings. Satan had blinded them to the truth. Then comes Jesus, "...He that is without sin among you, let him first cast a stone at her."[33]

"The very essence of spiritual warfare is lies versus truth. Satan and his angels go all out to get you to love their lies more than you love the truth of God."[34] Studying to show thyselves approved and seeking truth will be a great deterrent for the believer. Yet, it will not change the fact

---

[31] John 8:32, *Holy Bible KJV*, 1984

[32] Rom. 3:23, *Holy Bible KJV*, 1984

[33] John 8:7 KJV, *The Comparative Study Parallel Bible Presenting NIV, NASB, AMP, KJV*, 1984

[34] Beam, Joe, *Seeing the Unseen*, 2000, 13

that opposition will come. Since Satan comes to steal, kill and destroy, he will never give up. Being persistent is how he operates. Wearing down faith and trust with longsuffering more often ends in victory for the adversary.

“Follow the progression: Darkened understanding leads to a hardened heart; a hardened heart leads to lost sensitivity and an immersion in sensuality. (This is not a 'good sensuality' but one that indulges itself in every kind of impurity with a continual lust for more.) Reaching this point, the lie is believed. Having no communion with God, spiritual destruction results.

It's a simple strategy, and it's just as effective now as it has been throughout the history of the world. On this master template, Satan overlays varying strategies to mislead, confuse, deter, manipulate, and deceive.”[35]

---

[35] Beam, Joe, *Seeing the Unseen*, 2000, 13-14

Fear

Fear is known in the earth realm as false evidence appearing real by some while others choose to believe that they have no fear at all of anything. Satan uses fear to immobilize and tear down God's people by keeping them anxious with the what if's. What if the stock market crashes? What if the gas prices continue to soar? What if the doctor finds something...? on and on. "Do not be anxious about anything, but in everything, prayer and petition, with thanksgiving, present your request to God."[36]

God has not promised you tomorrow and yesterday is gone forever. Today is all that matters. However, people are caught up with knowing the future. This is nothing new. Since the olden days, kings and queens would solicit soothsayers, sorcerers, and even prophets to delve into their tomorrows. Today it is horoscopes, fortune tellers, psychics, tarot cards, and whatever else man can find. The forces of darkness thrive in this area and enjoys great success. If the focus stays on what's to come, then the attacks will come today.

Ambivalence and worry fuel the satanic fire that burns in

---

[36] Phil. 4:6 NIV, *The Comparative Study Parallel Bible Presenting NIV, NASB, AMP. KJV*, 1984

the hearts of mankind. The spirit of fear lurks about to destroy the believers as well as the unbelievers. This is why Paul writes, "For God has not given us the spirit of fear; but of power and of love and of a sound mind."[37]

"Fear is a fascinating subject because it has two sides. There is a negative side to fear in that it can paralyze us and tyrannize our lives. It can keep us from being all that God wants us to be. But fear also has a positive side. Fear is able to stimulate and motivate us to greatness. It-can drive us to do things we know God wants us to do with the life He has given us."[38]

Was it fear that caused Peter to get out of the boat? Was he more afraid of the storm or seeing Jesus walk on water? Was it fear that Jonah faced in the belly of the whale to go to Nineveh? Was it the fear of the fish or the fear of the Lord? The experiencing of fear comes to every life at one point or another. Discerning the positive or negative affect it has when it comes will be what makes the difference.

---

[37] 2 Tim. 1:7, *Holy Bible KJV*, 1984

[38] Young, Ed Jr., *Know Fear*, 2003, 3-4

Doubt

Doubt has been accused of being the opposite of fear in some circles. However, to doubt is to disbelieve or to waiver. It is an unsure state of mind. Therefore, faith which is to believe what is not as though it were, would be the opposite of doubt. Without trust there will be doubt.

Satan takes the stronghold of doubt and brings about confusion and God is not the author of confusion. The idea is to let the truth go forth. Plant a seed of dissension related to that truth. If that individual is not rooted and grounded in that truth that will evoke questions. A good example is Jesus and Satan in the wilderness.

Prior to Jesus' departure into the wilderness to be tempted of Satan, he had been baptized by John. "And lo a voice from heaven, saying, This is my beloved Son, in whom I am well pleased."[39] A proclamation had gone out before mankind and the tempter, that Jesus was, indeed, the Son of God. As soon as the forty day fast had ended, the enemy showed up with an agenda. Satan begins to question the deity of Jesus with "if thou be" in the Book of Matthew. However, there is no doubt in God. Everything is yes, no, and amen.

---

[39] Matt. 3:17, *Holy Bible KJV*, 1984

The enemy knew Jesus from Creation. The same way he attempted to question God's truth related to the Savior he does with mankind. If there is any doubt in you, it waivers your faith. This opens a door giving the enemy access to your power. "For verily I say unto you, that whosoever shall say unto this mountain, Be thou removed and be thou cast into the sea; and shall not doubt in his heart, but shall believe that those things which he saith shall come to pass; he shall have whatsoever he saith."[40]

---

[40] Mark 11 :23, *Holy Bible KJV*, 1984

Sin

"We may define sin as follows: Sin is any failure to conform to the moral law of God in act, attitude or nature. Sin here is defined in relationship to God and His moral law."[41] Sin is perhaps the deadliest tool in Satan's arsenal because it encompasses everything. It is the very foundation of evil. "Even before the disobedience of Adam and Eve, sin was present in the angelic world with the fall of Satan and demons."[42]

"The doctrine of sin is both extremely important because it affects and is also affected by many other areas of doctrine. Overview of the nature of God influences our understanding of sin."[43] Sin is a word known by young and old alike. However, many find it difficult to discuss it. Perhaps in doing so it causes the individual to look at themselves too closely. Mankind is known to have difficulty with objectively seeing themselves as sinners when in fact scripture says, "For all have sinned and come short of the glory of God."[44]

'When we say the soul is the natural life of man, we mean

---

[41] Gruden, Wayne, *Systematic Theology*. 1994, 490

[42] Gruden, Wayne, *Systematic Theology*. 1994, 492

[43] Erickson, Millard J., Christian Theology 2nd Edition, 2005, 580

[44] Rom. 3:23, *Holy Bible KJV*, 194

it is the power which preserves us alive in the flesh. Our soul is our life. This life is entirely distinct from the new life the Holy Spirit gives us at new birth. What the Holy Spirit imparts is God's uncreated life; this other is but man's created life.

Soul life supplies the energy for executing whatever is commanded. If the spirit rules, the soul will be directed by the spirit to exercise its volition to decide or to do on behalf of the spirit's desire; if, however sin reigns the body, the soul will be enticed by sin into using its volition to decide or to do what sin desires. The soul works according to its master, for its function is the execution of orders. Prior to man's fall it committed its power to the spirit's direction; but after the fall it responded completely to sin's coercion.

Because man turned into a fleshly being this sin which afterwards reigned in the body became man's nature, enslaving the soul and the life of man and compelling him to walk after sin. In this way sin became man's nature while soul became man's life."[45]

---

[45] Nee, Watchman, *The Spiritual Man*, Vols. 1-111, 1977, 142-143

Chapter IV: God's Weapons of Warfare

The Blood of Jesus

The Old Testament refers repeatedly to the atonement of the sins of man by the priest shedding the blood of an animal. Even then blood had to be shed annually just to cover sin. Never in that dispensation of time was the sin eradicated, merely covered. "For the life of the flesh is in the blood; and I have given it to you upon the altar to make an atonement for your souls; for it is the blood that maketh atonement for the soul."[46] Man knew that the blood had power even back to the Passover and the covering of doorposts to deter death.

No written words of man can better speak to the heart than the words offered in the Book of Hebrews 9:11-14 KJV. "But Christ being come as a High Priest of good things to come, by a greater and more perfect tabernacle, not made with hands, that is to say, not of this building; Neither by the blood of goats and calves, but by his own blood he entered in once into the holy place, having

---

[46] Lev. 17:11 KJV, *The Comparative Study Parallel Bible Presenting NIV. NASB. AMP. KJV*, 1984

obtained eternal redemption for us. For if the blood of bulls and of goats and the ashes of an heifer sprinkling the unclean, sanctifieth to the purifying of the flesh; How much more shall the blood of Christ who through the eternal Spirit offered himself without spot to God, purge your conscience from dead works to serve the living God?" Focusing in on verse twelve where it is noted he entered in once. Never will the blood of Christ be shed again. It took only one time to cover it all.

"No wonder Satan hates the blood. No wonder he is afraid of the blood. If he had known what he was doing, he would never have shed that innocent blood. But it was done 'once and for all,' and it can never be undone. He thought the crucifixion was his greatest victory, but it was actually his ultimate defeat."[47]

---

[47] Meyer, Joyce, *The Word the Name the Blood*, 1995, 112

The Word of God

"In the beginning was the Word and the Word was with God, and the Word was God...And the Word was made flesh and dwelt among us, (and we beheld his glory, the glory as of the only begotten of the Father,) full of grace and truth."[48] Everyday words are spoken. The believers know the significance of their words as the Bible declares. Out of your mouth come blessings or curses. Speak those things that are not as though they were. From the abundance of the heart, the mouth speaks. Think it not strange that the enemy knows the Word, as well. In some cases it may be justified in saying, perhaps, better than some Christians."

As previously in the scenario with Jesus and Satan in the wilderness, note how Satan quoted scripture to the Living Word. The lesson to be gleaned from this passage of scripture in this arena is this, the enemy knows the Word and how to manipulate and distort it to bring about confusion. The Bible talks about doctrines of devils, (I Tim 4:1), which are twisted, hollow, powerless words devised to overtake the belief system.

The Word being made flesh is absolute, therein no imperfections and the ability to never fail. Proof, that as

---

[48] John 1:1&14, *Holy Bible KJV*, 1984

it is written it can and has been done. It is through the Holy Spirit that the Word of God sustains its power. The Spirit being the mind of God acts on His behalf. In Ephesians6:17 "And take the helmet of salvation, and the sword of the Spirit, which is the Word of God." It is noted that the Word is a weapon with which one attacks an enemy. A sword in the sheath is of no value. It must be wielded or taken from the sheath and appropriately used. The Word of God is the believer's, and he must learn to apply it accurately."[49] God's Word is true knowledge of Him and His ways and character.

Paul tells Timothy to tell the church, "Study to shew thyself approved unto God, a workman that needeth not to be ashamed, rightly dividing the word of truth."[50] "Every day you should speak the Word, pray the Word, love the Word and honor the Word. The Word of God is the two-edged sword that is your weapon of offense with which you are able to defend yourself. If you keep your sword drawn, the enemy won't be as quick to approach you."[51]

[49] Meyer, Joyce, *The Word the Name the Blood*, 1995, 18-19

[50] 2 Tim. 2:15, *Holy Bible KJV*, 1984

[51] Meyer, Joyce, *The Word the Name the Blood*, 1995, 21

The Name of Jesus

In the Bible names were given for purpose and significance unlike in these modern days. Names of today may have no significance or importance. They just sound good. "Even in the very beginning of the Bible we see that names were tremendously important, for they described character."[52] There were instances when God even changed the name of some of His people because their circumstances changed. It is noted in Genesis Chapter 17 that Abram and Sarai had a name change because of a character change. Abram became Abraham the father of many nations and Sarai became Sarah the princess. Jacob became Israel because he would become the biological father of the twelve tribes and a prince." And he said, Thy name shall be called no more Jacob, but Israel for as a prince hast thou power with God and with men, and hast prevailed."[53]

Proverbs 22:1 says "A good name is rather to be chosen than great riches, and loving favor rather than silver and gold." Long after death a good name continues to live on. "A good name is better than precious ointment; and the day of death than the day of one's birth."[54]

---

[52] Meyer, Joyce, *The Word the Name the Blood*, 1995, 82

[53] Gen. 32:28, *Holy Bible KJV*, 1984

[54] Ecc. 7:1, *Holy Bible KJV*, 1984

There is power in the name of Jesus. As a weapon of warfare it is Almighty. There is victory in the name of Jesus. When Jesus entered into the country of the Gadarenes where the man possessed with the unclean spirit named Legion lived he saw Jesus from afar off. He rushed over, "And cried with a loud voice, and said, What have I to do with thee Jesus, thou Son of the most high God?" I adjure thee by God, that thou torment me not."[55] Another account of the enemy's recognition of the powerful name of Jesus, "And the evil spirit answered and said, Jesus I know and Paul I know, but who are ye?... And this was known to all the Jews and Greeks dwelling in Ephesus; and fear fell on them all and the name of the Lord Jesus... was magnified."[56]

The enemy has no power or authority over Jesus. After Jesus relinquished His earth suit and returned to His proper place at the right hand of the Father, Satan is rendered helpless. The cross, the blood resurrection and the name has re-established all that had been lost in the Garden of Eden. Bless the wonderful name of Jesus. For, it is the name above every name.

---

[55] Mark 5:7, *Holy Bible KJV*, 1984

[56] Acts 19:15&17, *Holy Bible KJV*, 1984

Faith

"Now faith is the substance of things hoped for, the evidence of things not seen."[57] It's not faith that's difficult. it's living by it. Faith is more than just believing that God exists. "And without faith it is impossible to please God, because anyone who comes to him must believe that he exists and that he rewards those who earnestly seek him."[58] Faith believes that God keeps His word, rewarding those who are His. Faith is trusting the promises you have no way to measure or authenticate until you receive. It's believing you have them when they aren't yet realities in the physical world."[59]

Faith is something that Christians speak of all the time. Some churches are called faith churches. So if faith is untouchable and unmeasurable, how do you become a faith church? Just how is faith acquired? The following two passages of scripture are very important in understanding faith. "Faith comes from hearing the message and the message is heard through the Word of Christ."[60] To be a church of faith is to study, teach and

---

[57] Heb. 1:1, *Holy Bible KJV*, 1984

[58] Heb. 11:6, *Holy Bible KJV*, 1984

[59] Beam, Joe, *Seeing the Unseen*, 2000, 303-304

[60] Rom. 10:17 NIV, *The Comparative Study Parallel Bible Presenting NIV. NASS, AMP. KJV*, 1984

believe. "The principle is that you believe in something you cannot see because you believe the message of the one who tells you it is there. The word of Jesus Christ is good testimony, believable and trustworthy"[61]

Paul says this, "For by grace given me I say to every one of you: Do not think of yourself more highly than you ought, but rather think of yourself with sober judgment, in accordance with the measure of faith God has given you."[62] The following three things have been previously noted in scripture.

1. God gives every man a measure of faith and to not get puffed-up because of the level of that faith. It is only by the unmerited grace of God was it given unto you.
2. The only way to increase in faith is by the hearing of the Word
3. Without faith it is impossible to please God.

Because every individual is different so then is their level of faith. Each trial increases the level of faith making some grow much faster than others. The more God's Holy Ghost power visibly works in the life of an individual the easier it becomes to trust God in unseen areas. Faith

---

[61] Beam,Joe, *Seeing the Unseen*, 2000, 304

[62] Rom. 12:3 NIV, *The Comparative Study Parallel Bible Presenting NIV, NASS, AMP, KJV*, 1984

building is like on-the-job training. It is encouraging to see God do a new thing in the lives of others because of faith. However, one is strengthened even the more when God moves for them.

Praise

The Word of God extols the saints of God to give praise. This weapon of warfare is so effective until it confuses the enemy. King Jehoshaphat was facing impendent doom. He knew his enemy was too great to defeat through the power of his might. Even though the king had called a fast throughout the land he was still afraid of the massive army of his enemy. The Word of God came upon Jahaziel, that the battle belonged to the Lord. Jehoshaphat sought God for guidance, and this is what happened, "And when he had consulted with the people, he appointed singers unto the Lord and that should praise the beauty of holiness, as they went out before the army and to say, Praise the Lord; for his mercy endureth forever. And when they began to sing and to praise, the Lord set ambushments against the children of Ammon, Moab, and Mount Seir which were come against Judah; and they were smitten."[63] David knew the significance of praise. The Book of Psalms is the book of praise. Scripture after scripture and verse upon verse is written in magnification of God.

Praise angers the enemy because his objective is either to steal, kill, or destroy. When he comes with full force, he cannot understand how you can raise your hands, or sing

---

[63] II Chr. 20:21-22, *Holy Bible KJV*, 1984

your song of praise even in the midst of adversity. It just does not make sense. Perhaps this Is why Paul says, "By him therefore let us offer the sacrifice of praise to God continually that is, the fruit of our lips giving thanks to his name."[64]

It is difficult to see the end result when there is trouble on every hand. The saved or unsaved can give praise when all is well. It is a sacrifice to press in the midst of adversity. This is when faith brings to mind that praise is the answer. An innocent life, shed blood, a cross and a risen Savior will never change. Praise is not up for questioning. It is a mandate to all living things that hath breath." Let everything that hath breath praise the Lord. Praise ye the Lord."[65] In all that God does expect a blessing to ensue. "But thou are holy. 0 thou that inhabitest the praises of Israel."[66]

Since God comes and dwells therein when praise is being offered as Paul said earlier, praise continually. Praise evokes the presence of the Lord. The more that praise is lifted before God the more blessings will be showered down. King David apparently got the revelation because he spent his life praising God.

---

[64] Heb. 13:15, *Holy Bible KJV*, 1984

[65] Psalm 150:6, *Holy Bible KJV*, 1984

[66] Psalm 22:30, *Holy Bible KJV*, 1984

Obedience

"The disease of evil is rooted in our hearts. The Bible is insistent about that, and there is no easy cure. Only Christ's blood, spilled from an innocent heart is sufficient to overcome its power. But even Christ's death does not free us - in the here and now - from the effects of evil."[67] Obedience is the key to pleasing God and walking upright. In order to obey there must be some type of guideline or rules to follow. The infallible words of God found in the Bible have been penned for just that reason.

Otherwise, each individual would set their own standards of living. The Word is clear-cut when it comes to the expectation of God....God's rules are designed either to protect us from harming ourselves, to keep us from hurting others, or to rescue us from wasting our lives."[68]

To obey Christ is to love Him and to love Him is to trust Him. Without love and trust in God, obedience will be virtually impossible. Throughout scripture God purposed individuals for difficult assignments with life threatening implications. As He does this modern-day love for the Savior has to supersede what is natural. In order to obey, a relationship is necessary between the speaker and the doer.

---

[67] Hybels, Bill & Wilkins, Rob, *Descending Into Greatness*, 1993, 146-147

[68] Hybels, Bill & Wilkins, Rob, *Descending Into Greatness*, 1993, 149

There has to be a strong bond between the two in order for dialogue. They would have to recognize one another. Trust plays a major role in this scenario because why obey anything or anyone in which you have no confidence. Loves causes the bond to be strengthened even the more.

Throughout scripture, this type of loving relationship is noted. There are too many incidents to list. Think upon these things. Three young men thrown into a fiery furnace because they loved God too much to obey any other God. Daniel was thrown in the den of lions because he refused to stop praying and praising God. Job was allowed to be tormented, but never stopped trusting. Stephen was stoned to death because he obeyed the call to share the good news. John the Baptist was beheaded, he who loved, trusted and obeyed the Lord even from the womb. This point being, to obey may mean to die. "Though he were a Son, yet learned he obedience by the things which he suffered; And being made perfect, he became the author of eternal salvation unto all them that obey him."[69] To do God's Will is better than any sacrifice man can make.

---

[69] Heb. 5:8-9, *Holy Bible KJV*, 1984

Worship

Worship (*PROSKUNEO*: Greek) is defined as an act of homage or reverence.[70]

"Whereas edification focuses on the believers and benefits them, worship concentrates on the Lord: Worship, the praise and exaltation of God, was a common Old Testament practice as can be seen particularly in the Book of Psalms."[71]

Praise and worship are closely related. Both give thanks to almighty God. Both are from the heart. However, there is a significant difference. A song writer once wrote, "Praise is what I do," but worship is who you are. As mentioned earlier, praise focuses on the believer, but worship on the Lord. Praise can be generated from the mind, will and emotions. But Jesus makes it perfectly clear, "God is a Spirit; and they that worship Him must worship Him in spirit and in truth."[72] After the flesh which is limited does and says what it can do to admonish God in praise then the spirit takes over. No wonder the Word says to worship the Lord in

---

[70] Vine, W.E., *Vine's Expository Dictionary of Old & New Testament Words*, 1997, 1247

[71] Erickson, Millard J., *Christian Theology* 2nd Edition, 2005. 1066

[72] John 4:24, *Holy Bible KJV*, 1984

spirit and note the word, truth. The spirit of the Lord in the believer is the mind of God in the person of the Holy Spirit. God then begins to connect with His own spirit. This causes a change in location for the believer. The worshipper is then spiritually transformed from the earth realm praise to spirit realm worship. When God connects with the Holy Spirit in you therein is truth, the whole truth and nothing but the truth. Jesus has already left on record, "I am the way, the truth and the life; no man cometh unto the Father, but by me."[73]

"We were created for God's pleasure. We were not created to live for ourselves but for Him. And while the Lord desires that we enjoy His gifts and His people, He would have us know we were created first for His pleasure. God finds His own reward for creating man. They are His worshippers. They are on earth only to please God, and when He is pleased, they also are pleased. The Lord takes them farther and through more pain and conflicts than other men. Outwardly, they often seem 'smitten of God, and afflicted.' {Isa. 53:4) Yet to God they are His beloved. When they are crushed, like the petals of a flower, they exude a worship, the fragrance of which is so beautiful and rare that angels weep in quiet awe at their surrender. They are the Lord's purpose for creation. And in the face of

---

[73] John 14:6, *Holy Bible KJV*, 1984

persecutions, their love and worship toward God became all consuming."[74]

True worship is a love for God in action.

---

[74] Frangipane, Francis, *The Three Battlegrounds*, 1989, 93-94

Prayer

"This question - what is prayer- has been asked many times over the years and has some very simple answers. Prayer is entering into communication with God - coming face to face with God."[75]

"If you are a Christian, there is power accompanying your life that is greater than great; the surpassing greatness of His power. It is not human power, but the actual strength of His might."[76] It has been said by E.M. Bounds, "Much prayer, much power, little prayer, little power and no prayer, no power." The key is to stay in constant communication with God. "As we truly, passionately and accurately submit to Christ in prayer, the kingdom of heaven steadily enters our non-prayed-for-world. The key, of course, is to know Christ's Word. We do not have authority; Christ has authority. What we have is revelation and submission. But as we submit to the Word, and persevere in prayer, the future is impacted and confirmed to God's Will."[77] Perhaps, this is why Jesus stayed in constant communication with the Father. Scripture tells us to do likewise "Pray without ceasing."[78]

---

[75] Pollard, Mark, *It's Prayer Time!*, 2000, 40

[76] Frangipane, Francis, *Prayer*, 2004, 18

[77] Frangipane, Francis, *Prayer*, 2004, 19

[78] I Thes. 5:17, *Holy Bible KJV*, 1984

Many may question within their heart just what does prayer accomplish? "On the one hand, if prayer has any sense depends on or is altered by whether and how much someone prays. On the other hand, if God's plan is established and He will do what He is going to do then does it matter whether we pray?"[79]

"Prayer as combined with the Word, is also a universal means of grace. When the promises of the Word are pleaded in prayer, they become effective in the spiritual life of the Christian. Prayer as defined by Mr. Watson is "The offering of our desires to God through the mediation of Jesus Christ, under the influences of the Holy Spirit, and with suitable dispositions for things agreeable to His will." Thus, to be acceptable to God, prayer must be offered through mediation of Christ; must be offered in faith and in a spirit of humility; and must be according to the will of God. The elements of a well- ordered prayer include adoration, which ascribes to God the perfections which belong to His nature, and which should be uttered in deep devotion, reverence, confidence, and affection; thanksgiving, or the pouring forth of the soul in gratitude; confession, or deep penitence, submission, and humility; supplication, or a prolonged and earnest looking to God in dependence for needed blessings; and intercession, or

---

[79] Erickson, Millard J., *Christian Theology* 2nd Edition, 2005, 430

a pleasing for our fellowmen, with sincere desires for their spiritual welfare (cf. I Timothy 2:1). Prayer is an obligation, a duty upon all men in private, in the family, and in public. If it be neglected or omitted, there can be no advance in spiritual things."[80]

---

[80] Wiley, H. Orton, S.T.D. & Culbertson, Paul T., Ph.D., *Introduction to Christian Theology*, 1946, 385

Chapter V: Victorious in Battle

More than Conquerors

To be more than conquerors is a bold statement coming from Paul, "Nay in all these things we are more than conquerors through him that loved us."[81] The question arises, all of what things? In the preceding verses, reference is made about tribulation, distress, persecution, famine, nakedness, peril, sword, etc. He then goes on to say that no matter what comes or goes in heaven or earth, the only objective is to love God through Jesus. Paul is asserting that through Jesus there is victory in all things. No matter how intense or overwhelming, the answer lies in Jesus.

More than implies there will always be residual after each task, fight or assignment. When it seems all hope is gone and strength exhausted, somehow there is just a little bit more. The Holy Spirit works to motivate and to encourage in times of trouble. For the victory does not come through the power and might of man but through the power and might of Almighty God.

Job is the perfect example of being more than a

---

[81] Rom. 8:37, *Holy Bible KJV*, 1984

conqueror. Many of the trials he faced would be incomprehensible to most. Each time, with each loss, he stood his ground. In the midst of adversity, Job kept his integrity. He conquered one setback after another. Through Christ Jesus there is no failure and no defeat. Be comforted and rest assured, for it has been left on record, "But they that wait upon the Lord shall renew their strength; they shall mount up with wings as eagles; they shall run, and not be weary; and they shall walk; and not faint.[82] The victory comes through the trusting and the waiting.

---

[82] Isa. 40:31, *Holy Bible KJV*, 1984

Overcomers

To be an overcomer means to win, to ultimately win.

"There was a multitude on Golgotha who attended the crucifixion of men and who actually heard their cries when nails were hammered into their hands and feet. They must have known that at least one of them was the best of men. Otherwise He would not have prayed for His torturers or cared to bring a robber to God, while passing through unspeakable physical suffering himself."[83]

Everyone knows to serve Jesus costs something. Perhaps this may be why so many reject God. The Lord knew in order to overcome the things of the world would be at a great cost. He was more focused on the gain. The shedding of His blood for the remission of sin and redeeming that which was without hope and lost was His mission. Paul writes, "For Christ Jesus my Lord; I have suffered the loss of all things and do count them but dung, that I may win Christ."[84]

To overcome the things of this world is to overcome the ruler of this world. He uses every strategy known to man to counteract obedience. King David knew, Job knew,

---

[83] Wurmbrand, Richard, *The Overcomers*, 2006, 272

[84] Wurmbrand, Richard, *The Overcomers*, 2006, 273

Paul knew and everyone who died in Christ had the revelation that obedience is the key to being a true overcomer. Jesus says it better than anyone in the following scriptures, "... To him that overcometh will I give to eat of the tree of life, which is in the midst of the paradise of God."[85] And he that overcometh and keepeth my works unto the end, to him will I give power over the nations."[86] Finally, that man may know that when the fight of faith has been fought and the warfare ceases, Jesus' promise is this, "To him that overcometh will I grant to sit with me in my throne, even as I also overcame and am set down with my Father in his throne."[87] Hallelujah!!!

[85] Rev. 2:7, *Holy Bible KJV*, 1984

[86] Rev. 2:26, *Holy Bible KJV*, 1984

[87] Rev. 3:21, *Holy Bible KJV*, 1984

Conclusion

This writing was intended to prick the heart and mind of the children of God. This is in an effort to uncover, so to speak, some pitfalls or kinks in your armor rendering you ineffective in battle. As you continue to read on prayerfully, thought provoking questions should arise.

Some say the Bible is basic instructions before leaving earth. Though secular in origin, this statement is quite true. The Bible paints the picture of God's plan and purpose for all of mankind and his creation. The plan was perfect and perfected in the mind of an almighty God. Had this plan been implemented without the component of the freedom of choice, oooh weee! However, without the ability to choose of our own volition God would have been the Master and not the Father.

As was pointed out here and throughout the Word even the angels had a choice. Serving God was not Satan's choice, and this is revealed all the way back to the beginning in the Book of Genesis. But, because of the sovereignty of God and his faith and love in mankind, Satan lives.

Many believers live their lives daily completely oblivious to these implications of unrest in the spirit realm.

It is safe to say that the adversary hates God and the things of God. He seeks to steal, kill, and destroy. Jesus said that the world hated him first suggesting that the world would hate you, too. These words have been penned to remind the children of God. Though we battle daily the things of the world, all things have been conquered and overcome by the Lamb of God.

Ignorance is not bliss and what you don't know can not only hurt you but kill you. The enemy thrives on the ignorance of man. Warfare is prevalent at all times in all lives. That's life. Whether you choose to acknowledge it is where the devil has the upper hand. Through deception, lies, and sin it appears that he wins. However, let the record show that the devil is a liar.

The tempter is skilled in the art of war but so are you. His devices are designed specifically for each individual. He studies each opponent to discern weaknesses, insecurities, and ways to gain access into the database as to ultimately destroy the main frame. Fear not, God has supplied a way of escape. Satan knows that he has already been defeated and his time is running out. The master plan is to keep the saints so bogged down with the little things so the focus cannot be on the first estate. Glorifying God and building the kingdom is the ultimate goal.

If in the process of reading these pages an epiphany has occurred in the mind of God's elect, it has accomplished its purpose. Henceforth now and forever more question everything that does not line up with God's Word. Watch as well as pray. Pray in season and out of season. Be ready to stand, fully clothed in the proper attire. Keep your mind stayed on heavenly things. Study to show thyself approved. Use the tools that God has provided for the battle. Realize you have been given power and authority over all the wiles of the enemy.

When confronted with a fight stop whining and go into attack mode. Jesus did this in the wilderness when the tempter confronted Him. Lest it be God's Will to perfect the gifts in you, some things, believers do not have to accept. Why continuously fight sickness when by Jesus' stripes you are healed. Why struggle in lack when God said He would supply you every need according to his riches in glory? Why give up when you cannot see change? "Now faith is the substance of things hoped for, the evidence of things not seen."[88] Know and understand that God has equipped each and every one to complete the assignment for which they were purposed. The fight is lost in the preparation. Today is a good day to prepare for the warfare ahead. Fight the good fight of faith because at the end of the Book of Revelation it says you win.

---

[88] Heb. 11:1, *Holy Bible KJV*, 1984

Bibliography

Beam, Joe. Seeing the *Unseen*. West Monroe, LA: Howard Publishing Co., Inc., 2000

Erickson, Millard J. *Christian Theology* 2nd Edition. Grand Rapids, MI: Baker Academic, 2005

Frangipane, Francis. *Prayer*. Cedar Rapids, IA: Arrow Publications, Inc., 2004

Frangipane, Francis. *The Power of One Christ Like Life*. New Kensington, PA: Whitaker House, 1999, 2000

Frangipane, Francis. *The Three Battlegrounds* Cedar Rapids, IA: Arrow Publications, 1989

Geisler, Dr, Norman. *Systematic Theology*. Minneapolis, MN: Bethany House, 2002

Gills, James P, M.D. and Heartlight. *The Unseen Essential*. Tarpon Springs, FL: Love Press, 1990

Gruden, Wayne. *Systematic Theology*. Grand Rapids, MI: Zondervan Publishing House, 1994

Guralnik, David and Hinze, *Richard H. Webster's New World Dictionary and Student Handbook*, Elementary Edition. Nashville, TN: Southwestern Company, 1966

Hybels, Bill and Wilkins, Rob. *Descending Into Greatness*. Grand Rapids, MI: Zondervan Publishing House, 1993

Jeffrey, Grant R. *Heaven The Mystery of Angels*. Toronto, Ontario: Frontier Research Publications, Inc., 1996

Kirsch, Jonathan. *God Against the Gods*. New York, NY: Penguin Group, 2004

Lucado, Max. *In the Eye of the Storm*. Dallas-London-Vancouver-Melbourne: Word Publishing, 1991

Lucado, Max. *Traveling Light*. Dallas-London-Vancouver-Melbourne: Word Publishing, 2001

McQuilkin, Robertson. *Life In the Spirit*. Nashville, TN: Broadman & Holman, 2000

Meyer, Joyce. *The Word the Name The Blood*. Tulsa, OK: Harrison House, Inc., 1995

Nee, Watchman. The Spiritual *Man*, Vols. 1-111. New York, NY: Christian Fellowship Publishers, Inc., Reprinted as Combined Edition, 1977

Newcombe, Jerry and Kristi. *A Way of Escape*. Nashville, TN: Broadman & Holman Publishers, 1999

Page, Sydney H.T. *Powers of Evil*. Grand Rapids, MI: Baker Books, 1995

Peretti, Frank E. *This Present Darkness*. Westchester, IL: Good News Publishers, 1986

Pollard, Mark. *It's Prayer Time!* Ventura, CA: Regal Books, 2000

Roberts, Frances J. *Come Away My Beloved*. Uhrichville, OH: Barbour Publishing, Inc., 2002

Trimm, Dr. N. Cindy. *The Rules of Engagement Workbook*. Ft. Lauderdale, FL: Kingdom Life Publishing Co., 2001

Vine, W.E. *Vine's Expository Dictionary of Old & New Testament Words*. Nashville, TN: Thomas Nelson Publishers, 1997

Wrigglesworth, Smith. *Greater Works, Experiencing God's Power*. New Kensington, PA: Whitaker House, 1999

Wiley, H. Orton, S.T.D. *Christian Theology Vol. III*. Kansas City, MO: Beacon Hill Press, 1943

Wiley, H. Orton, S.T.D. and Culbertson, Paul T., Ph.D. *Introduction to Christian Theology*. Kansas City, MO: Beacon Hill Press, 1946

Wurmbrand, Richard. *The Overcomers*. Orlando, FL: Bridge-Logos 2006

Young, Ed Jr. *Know Fear*. Nashville, TN: Broadman & Holman, 2003

Reference Books

Holy Bible K.J.V. Nashville-Camden-New York: Thomas Nelson Publishers, 1984

The Comparative Study Parallel Bible Presenting N.I.V., N.A.S.B., A.M.P., K.J.V. Grand Rapids, MI: Zondervan Corp., 1984

Strong, James. *The New Strong's Exhaustive Concordance of the Bible*. Nashville, TN: Thomas Nelson Publishers, 1990

Man: God's Greatest Miracle

By Dr. Sonoma Carney Suggs, PhD

In Fulfillment of the PhD in Christian Education

Emanuel Theological Seminary

May 2015

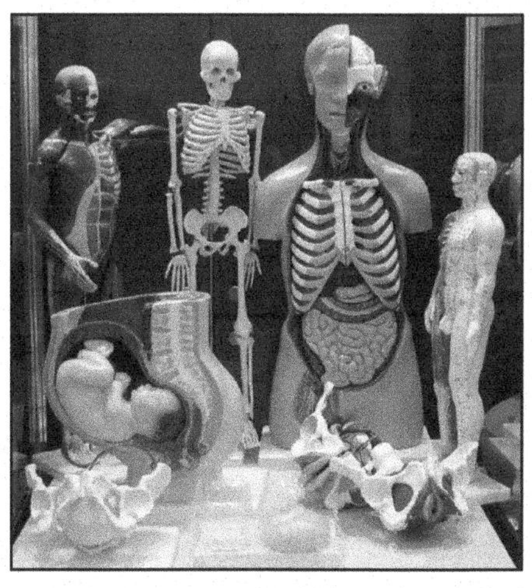

Introduction

Since the world was formed, people have searched for God's greatest miracle.

Regardless the cost or consequence the quest to find the most mystical makings of the Master has been the focus for thousands of years.

Does God's greatest accomplishment lie in the carvings of rock found at the foot of the Grand Canyon? Perhaps to some the majesty of the perfect sunset on any given day is unbelievable and incomprehensible. Yet others may marvel at each drop of water that collaborates one with another cascading down the mountain slope in perfect unity in what we have come to call Niagara Falls.

All that the Creator has made is miraculous and unique in every way. The handiwork of Almighty God is simply amazing and bears His signature. However, there is but one creation that encompasses His essence and is made in His image. Man is a living and breathing facsimile of greatness; scooped from the dirt and made to live forever...God's greatest miracle!

It sounds good to those with like views and ideology, but it would be amiss to believe that everybody believes, just because you do. One would first have to believe that God exists. Of course, the atheist would say that's not true. Then one would have to believe in creation. Well, it is known by many that Mr. Charles Darwin's Theory of Evolution refutes that.

"Lamarck was the first man whose conclusion on the subject excited much attention. This justly celebrated naturalist first published views in 1801. In these works, he upholds the doctrine that all species, including man are descended from other species. He first did the eminent service of arousing attention to the probability of all change in the organic as well as the inorganic world, being the result of law, and not of miraculous interposition."[1]

So just exactly what is the purpose behind these written words? As you proceed, note that the following words are merely to evoke thought, challenge your mindset, enlighten your intellect, and to delve deeper into the confines of the man in the mirror. It is the hope that the realization of who God has created you to be will establish a relationship between the Creator and the created; beyond anything the human mind could ever hope, think, dream, or even imagine.

---

[1] McHenry, Robert. *Charles Darwin The Origin of Species by Means of Natural Selection: Encyclopedia Britannica, Inc.*, 1952.

Chapter I: Body Works

In order to see man as God's greatest miracle an overview of his make-up is absolutely necessary. "And God said, Let us make man in our image. after our likeness:"[2] This passage of scripture, from Genesis 1:26a KJV, alludes that man was not just randomly created but specifically by intelligence far greater than some cataclysmic occurrence.

The human body is specific in every way.

"The human body is divided into four large anatomical areas: head, trunk, upper, and limbs. These areas are further divided into sub regions. They are all connected by complex joints that allow them to move in an independent manner."[3]

This mean machine is relentless yet delicate. It has to be nurtured and nourished in order to thrive and survive. Though it is but one body it is comprised of many members. Each member has an assignment. If at any time

---

[2] *Holy Bible KJV*: Zondervan Corp, 1984.

[3] Podesta, Martine. *The Ultimate Medical Encyclopedia*: Firefly, 2010, 40.

a member is compromised, the brain, which is the mastermind, assesses the situation. After a thorough investigation, it then calls on the appropriate members to handle the problem. For example, if an individual is choking, the signal to cough is sent to the respiratory system. "Coughing is a protective reflex to clear the trachea, bronchi, and lungs of irritants and secretions."[4]

There are so many wonderful, miraculous things concerning the body that it is difficult to find a focal point. Man stands on a base called feet. The feet are, of course, used for mobility, but they are mainly used for holding up the framework. They come in different sizes to accommodate the weight above them. There are five toes on each which account for balance because they spread to keep you upright while standing or walking.

The eyes enable us to see close up and at a distance, giving the brain time to survey your surroundings. They are located at the highest point of the face, which enhances the ability to see further. The eyes are able to see ahead but also peripherally. The eyes are covered with what are known as eyelids. Their job is to prevent debris from entering the eye. They are involuntary, which means they protect your eyes without you telling them to. The eye lashes are purposeful because, if, by chance,

---

[4] Potter, Patricia, and Perry, Ann Griffin: *Fundamentals of Nursing*: Mosley, INC., 2005, 1084.

any trash gets close enough it is caught in the lashes before it can enter the eye.

A few years back, it was all the rave to have a surround sound system on your television or stereo. However, the human body has always had one. The ears are located on both sides of the skull; not for decoration but that you might hear from all angles without turning around.

What is the purpose of the nose? Well, the nose is part of the respiratory system. Its job is to pull in the air from the atmosphere, which is then received down the trachea or windpipe, then sent to the lungs. The nose is located in the middle of your face, right above the mouth, which has a dual role. The mouth is part of the digestive system, but air is also exchanged through the mouth. Note, that as the eyes have lashes, the nose has cilia. Cilia is hair that functions in like manner to protect theses orifices from trash and debris. These tiny bits of information are just the tip of the iceberg. The following pages will give you an idea of how complex man really is. If the outer frame is as complicated as it appears, just imagine what the internal workings are like.[5]

---

[5] Podesta, Martine. *The Ultimate Medical Encyclopedia*: Firefly, 2010, 38-39.

Overview of The Systems

No matter what you are and how you arrived on the scene, one can see that the human body is more in depth than a simple life form. Somewhere in the back of your mind, questions should arise for which there may not be an explanation.

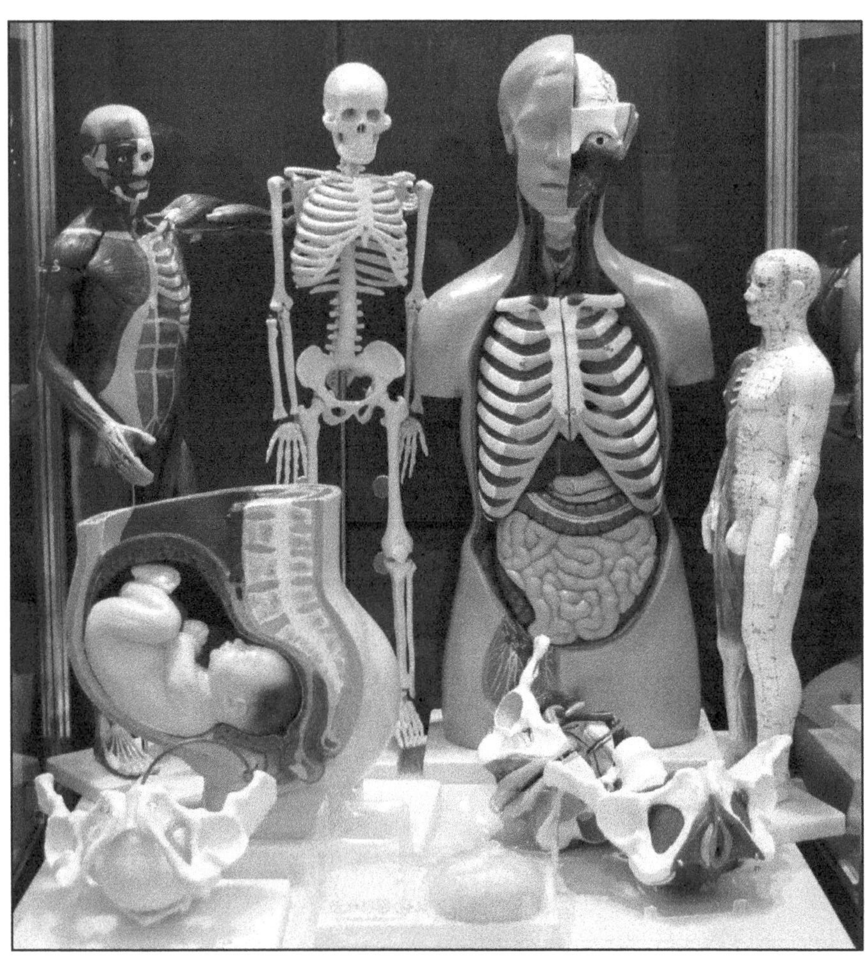

How does the kidney know how much potassium or magnesium to release during urination? Why do males have one less rib than females? How does the liver or kidney know how much of your medication to absorb, or what system to send it to, to maximize the best treatment for your issues? Let the record show that you do not have to be a scholar to realize, it's complicated.

The word "body" is not just applied to the human frame, but it is also used by God to identify the believers and followers of Christ. This is a nugget for thought even to the non-believer. *"For as the body is one, and hath many members, and all the members of that one body, being many, are one body: so also is Christ"*[6] I Corinthians 12:12 KJV.

---

[6] *Holy Bible KJV*: Thomas Nelson Publishers, 1984.

Chapter II: Brain...The Mainframe

August 2007 issue of Discovery Magazine stated:

"Of all the objects in the universe, the human brain is the most complex. There are as many neurons in the brain as there are stars in the Milky Way galaxy... It is likely that mental information is stored not in single cells but in populations of cells and patterns of their activity. However, it is currently not clear how to know which neurons belong to a particular group; worse still, current technologies (like sticking fine electrodes directly into the brain) are not well suited to measuring several thousand neurons at once. Nor is it simple to monitor the connections of even one neuron. A typical neuron in the cortex receives input from some ten thousand other neurons."[7]

It is no wonder that everything that happens to man starts in the mind. *"Let this mind be in you which was also in Christ Jesus."*[8] Philippians 2:5 KJV. Paul says think like

---

[7] Internet David Eagleman "10 Unsolved Mysteries of the Brain," Discovery Magazine, August 2007, http:/ /discovermagazine.com/2007/aug/unsolved-brain-mysteries.

[8] *Holy Bible KJV*: Thomas Nelson Publishers, 1984.

Jesus and things will work out, otherwise, who's to say how things will end up. When you stop to think it makes sense. If you are made in the image of God and He breathed His essence into you, thinking like Him would empower you over all sin and evil.

The brain is definitely the mastermind with its complicated workings. It has been said that man only uses 10% of his brain power and yet one could be considered a genius. It is hard to fathom what it would be like to operate at 50% or even 100%. Unless we are able to take our brain power and channel it into thinking like Jesus, it could be disastrous. What does that mean?

"Our actions are a direct result of our thoughts. If we have a negative mind, we will have a negative life."[9]

Though the brain is awesome it is easily manipulated by environment, unhealthy desires, emotions and a host of many more. God says in His word, *"For as a man thinketh in his heart, so is he."*[10] Proverbs 23:7 KJV.

"The mind is the battlefield. It is a vital necessity that we

---

[9] Meyers, Joyce, *Battlefield of the Mind: Winning the Battle of Your Mind.* New York, New York; Faith Words Hatchette Book Group, 1995, 3.

[10] *Holy Bible KJV*: Thomas Nelson Publishers, 1984.

line up our thoughts with God's thoughts."[11]

In chapter two of Genesis, God brings every living creature that He had created before Adam and whatever he called it, that was its name. Wow! How did he remember? How long did it take? God said every living creature from the earth. By the time chapter three ends and a few bad decisions later, Adam and Eve had been kicked out of the garden; man is fallen and now is given a mandate that he will die. What happened? You may say Satan. Not! He manipulates and instigates but he cannot make you do anything. The decision or choice must be your own. This is the first incident recorded of man's stinking thinking. After Adam got the wife and was in charge of everything, along comes Satan to offer him more. He had everything, and then he wanted to be a god. It seems that the more things change, the more they stay the same.

In this present time, that same concept remains alive and well. Of all the living things on this planet man is the ultimate creation and all God requires is that the created would live for the Creator. Mankind strives to live for himself in many instances, which separates him from God. As previously stated, man is one body with many

---

[11] Meyers, Joyce, *Battlefield of the Mind: Winning the Battle of Your Mind.* New York, New York; Faith Words Hatchette Book Group, 1995, 4.

members. The brain may be in charge of the thoughts, but the rest of the members have a say in the process as well. Your feet do not have to go in that direction, your eyes do not have to look at it, and your mouth does not have to say it. There is a way of escape. It does not mean that the brain will be overthrown; it simply means that with help from the members, the brain can be directed into choosing a better way.

"For no temptation-no trial regarded as enticing to sin [no matter how it comes or where it leads]- has overtaken you and laid hold on you that is not common to man-that is, no temptation or trial has come to you that is beyond human resistance and that is not adjusted and adapted and belonging to human experience, and such as man can hear. But God is faithful [to His word and to His compassionate nature], and He [can be trusted] not to let you be tempted and tried and assayed beyond your ability and strength of resistance and power to endure, but with the temptation He will [always] also provide the way out-the means of escape to a landing place- that you may be capable and strong and powerful, patiently to bear up under it."[12] I Corinthians 1O: 13.

It has been said that an idle mind is the devil's workshop. This is a statement that can be considered to be

---

[12] *The Comparative Study Bible*: Zondervan, 1984.

absolutely true. When the thoughts are allowed to wander, the enemy can plant seeds of doubt or distention. God said to just believe. When the what if's set in it opens the door to fear and a host of negative feelings and emotions. Satan knows that faith moves the heart of God. So he presents distractions which may eventually cause an individual to lose focus.

The above Scripture alludes to the fact that in life temptations will come, and that is normal to man. However, the good news is that God will give you the power and a way of escape.

Chapter III: The Heart of the Matter

When speaking of the heart, one would automatically focus on the physical heart. That makes sense; however, as you proceed there may be a change in perception.

"If you imagine that you are your body, you will experience life as an expression of the body. When you understand that you are your soul, then you will experience life as an expression of the soul. When you acknowledge that your soul and God's are one, then you will experience life as an expression of the One Spirit."[13]

God created man, not only to have dominion over the earth but to have communion with Him. God desires a relationship with His greatest creation. It is the Father's desire to be an intricate part of the matrix of man. However, how could an infinite, omnipotent God communicate with a finite mortal? The Bible declares that God says His ways are not man's ways and His thoughts are higher than the thoughts of man. So the Lord created man in His own image, with His essence as a way to stay connected and to communicate one with the other.

---

[13] Walsch, Donald Neale. Communion With God. New York, New York: G.P. Putnam's Sons, 2000, 190.

The heart is the spirit within man that connects mankind to his heavenly Father. When Donnie McClurkin sings his song *"Speak to My Heart"* (1996), he is inviting the Holy Spirit to converse with the part of him that will hear. You may think that because you have ears, you should automatically hear. As you will learn in chapter five, that is not always the case.

Joyce Meyers says it this way:

"The Mind of the Flesh versus The Mind of the Spirit [For those who are according to flesh and are controlled by its unholy desires, set their minds on and pursue those things which gratify the flesh, but those who are according to the Spirit and are controlled by the desires of the Spirit. set their minds on and seek those things which gratify the [Holy] Spirit. Romans 8:5"[14]

In simple terms, God says He has no intentions of talking to your flesh because it is evil, selfish and a host of other things. He gears the conversation toward the part of you that can appropriately hear and respond. "God is a Spirit: and they that worship Him must worship Him in spirit and

---

[14] Meyers, Joyce, *Battlefield of the Mind: Winning the Battle of Your Mind.* New York, New York; Faith
Words Hatchette Book Group, 1995, 19.

truth."[15] John 4:24 KJV. Man has a bad habit of rushing into situations and circumstances purely based on what they see and hear in the flesh. If one would take a moment for the Spirit of God to connect with their spirit (heart), God reveals Himself. "But the Lord said unto Samuel, Look not on his countenance or on the height of his stature; because I have refused him; for the Lord seeth not as man seeth, for man looketh on the outward appearance, but the Lord looketh on the heart." I Samuel 16:7 KJV.

Walking in the Spirit of the Lord is a game changer. As stated in The Fundamentals of Nursing:

"Health care research now shows the association between spirituality and health. There may be beneficial health outcomes when an individual is able to engage his or her beliefs in a higher power and sense a source of strength or support. The healing power of prayer may lower blood pressure (Koenig and others, 1997), reduce stress before surgery (Saudia and others, 1991), enhance cancer treatment (Lambe and others, 1996), or relieve depression and improve immune status in acquired immune deficiency syndrome (AIDS) clients (Adair and others, 1991; Carson and Green, 1992)..... The relationship between spirituality and healing is not

---

[15] *The Comparative Study Parallel Bible*: Zondervan Corp., 1984.

completely understood. However, it is the individual's intrinsic spirit that seems to be an important factor in healing...... There is a link between mind, body, and spirit. An individual's belief and expectations can and do have effects on the person's physical well-being."[16]

From the above information, it is not totally understood how just believing that God is able, can have a tremendous impact on their medical outcome. *"For as a man thinketh in his heart, so is he."*[17] Proverbs 23.7a KJV.

As you proceed into the pages to come you will note that many supernatural incidents occurred when individuals were walking in the Spirit of God. Peter walked on water. Enoch walked from one dimension into another without dying. *"And Enoch walked with God: and he was not found; for God took him."*[18] Genesis 5: 24 KJV. Abraham and Sarah conceived Isaac well beyond childbearing age. Elijah called down fire from heaven to defeat the prophets of Baal. The three Hebrew boys escaped fire and death in the fiery furnace. Daniel made it known that he had done no wrong and God delivered him from the lion's den.

---

[16] Potter, Patricia, and Perry, Anne Griffin: *Fundamentals of Nursing*: Mosley Inc., 2005, 545.

[17] *Holy Bible KJV*: Thomas Nelson Publishers, 1984.

[18] *Holy Bible KJV*: Thomas Nelson Publishers, 1984.

"My God hath sent His angel and hath shut the lion's mouths so that they have not hurt me; and as before him innocence was found in me; and also before thee, 0 king, have I done no hurt." Daniel 6:22 KJV.[19]

The Holy Scriptures list one account after another, from Genesis to Revelation about the power that God releases on His people when they walk in the Spirit. When man's heart is right with God, then he can truly do all things through Christ as the Bible declares. However, the enemy knows the same information and will try to make you think that it is about mankind. The connection to the power source becomes jeopardized when man forgets.

"Not by might, nor by power, but by my Spirit, saith the Lord of hosts."[20] Zechariah 4:6b

---

[19] *Holy Bible KJV*: Thomas Nelson Publishers, 1984.

[20] *Holy Bible KJV*: Thomas Nelson Publishers, 1984.

Chapter IV: See Your Way

When speaking of seeing, your mind automatically thinks of the eyes. Anatomically it is true that man has two eyes and the main purpose for them is to see. They are located at the highest point on the face below the forehead. Placed purposely and specifically for optimum service seems to have been the original plan. Yet there are many reasons why the eyes may not function properly. Some people are born with impaired vision or blindness. Others may just see partially through a dim glass and others may be seeing and see not. In other words, their eyes just might be wide shut.

Reverend Dr. Jennie B. Vaughn said frequently, "Everybody has two sets of eyes." As the years progressed and much teaching ensued, come to find out it was a reference to the natural and spiritual set of eyes. People from Missouri may say 'show me' while others may say 'seeing is believing'. It is not difficult at all to understand the natural function of the eye.

However, what is the purpose for the spiritual eyes? Is there such a thing as spiritual eyes? This is what Jesus says on the matter,

"For this people's heart has waxed gross, and their ears are dull of hearing, and their eyes they have closed; lest at any time they should see with their eyes, and hear with their ears, and should understand with their heart, and should be converted and I should heal them." Matthew 13:15 KJV[21]

Outside forces and circumstances can play an important role in not seeing clearly. From the spoken words of Jesus Christ it seems there may be something to the existence of spiritual eyes. Upon delving- deeper into the above passage of scripture, it seems to be a choice whether or not an individual desires to take advantage of this God given gift. Perhaps Reverend Dr. Vaughn was right. Everybody has the ability and just chooses not to use it.

Make no mistake about this gift to see beyond what is seen, God gave it and his gifts are without repentance. However, there are many manipulative outside forces that can distort, camouflage, imitate, and present illusions and hallucinations, vain imaginations, and many, many more. The brain is an intricate piece of this puzzle because this is where the fight takes place. To see beyond the natural is a choice the individual may not want to make, therefore, in seeing they see not. The English language has several words to describe this choice, such

---

[21] *Holy Bible KJV*: Thomas Nelson Publishers, 1984.

as perception, opinion, spiritual discernment. belief, etc. While you may choose to say half full, someone else says half empty. The fact is that either way, the content never changed. Jesus says, until you understand in your heart, your spirit man, your perspective will not change.

Elisha was a prophet also known as a seer. When he was focused completely on God he could see and hear things others could not. The gift of seeing in the spirit is priceless. Being able to see what God sees can protect you from harm, save others, head off imminent dangers and even prepare you for future events. Elisha's enemies had snuck up on him and his servant. When the servant saw the enemy coming, in fear, he ran back to tell his master. This is what transpired, "And he answered, Fear not; for they that be with us are more than they that be with them. And Elisha prayed, and said, Lord, I pray thee, open his eyes, that he may see.

"And the Lord opened the eyes of the young man; and he saw; and behold, the mountain was full of horses and chariots of fire round about Elisha."[22] II Kings 6:16-17 KJV.

What a gift. Notice that God opened the eyes of the young man. Historical accounts of God opening the eyes of other living species, is unavailable at this time. There

---

[22] *The Comparative Study Parallel Bible*: Zondervan Corp, 1984.

are many accounts of man's spiritual eyes being used in many forms and fashions. Joseph and Daniel could see through dreams. Ezekiel had visions when he saw wheels in the middle of wheels and dead dry bones coming back to life.

Even today, our modern society is riddled with dreams and visions of man; that have come to fruition. Laptops, electronic cars, smart phones, and microwaves are just examples of seeing in the spirit, beyond what others see. The good part about this miraculous gift that man possesses, is that it is free and life changing. Jesus declares that as long as you line up with His word, you will exude light because you will see Him. *"The light of the body is the eye: if therefore thine eye be single, thy whole body shall be full of light."*[23] Matthew 6:22 KJV

No one is capable of relying heavily on the eyes. Sometimes it seems as though our eyes play tricks on us. If we would only trust in what God says and not be listeners of the world, then our lives would be better. Our futures would then line up with God's will and God's ways.

---

[23] *Holy Bible KJV*: Thomas Nelson Publishers, 1984.

Chapter V: Listening Now and Hearing Later

"He that hath ears to hear let him hear."[24] Matthew 11:15 KJV

Looking at the human body as a miracle continues. In the above scripture Jesus makes a profound statement. Sounds like an oxymoron. If ears are meant to hear, then do something to make them hear. What is Jesus saying? Would any other species on earth be able to grasp the concept behind this command? Whatever it means it must be important because the Savior repeats this declaration over and over again in the New Testament books all the way to Revelation prior to His pre-stated return.

Anatomically man has two ears and unless they are impaired in some way their main function among others is to hear. Are you listening? As in the case of seeing not, these statements have moved beyond the physical realm to the spiritual one.

---

[24] *Holy Bible KJV*: Thomas Nelson Publishers, 1984.

Remember in chapter three, while discussing Matters of the Heart, it was proposed that the issue was not invoking the physical three-pound organ, but man's spiritual connection to God's spirit. It is in that place that God speaks into His own essence which He breathed into man causing him to become a living soul. When the Creator speaks to the created, he hears in the spirit man.

On a daily basis an individual is bombarded with several sounds at the same time.

Whether the birds are chirping, the clock is ticking, the television going, or the phone is ringing; subconsciously your ears are listening. However, would you be able to recall spiritually everything that was actually heard? Unless there is a spiritual connection, you can listen all day long and never hear.

Jesus does not need anyone to speak for Him. Yet, throughout scripture, He made it plain that the reason He chose to speak in parables at times, was to hide the kingdom principles from non-believers. The Pharisees and the scribes had itching ears, so they followed along in the crowds lurking and listening. Even though they were there, they still did not get it. *"My sheep hear my voice and I know them, and they follow me,"*[25] John 10:27 KJV

---

[25] *Holy Bible KJV*: Thomas Nelson Publishers, 1984.

God, being a sovereign God and a loving Father can open the ears of anything, anytime He chooses. He watches over His creation at all times and when necessary, He will speak in such a way that even without ears you can hear Him. For example, manna was commanded to fall from Heaven. The grave clothes that held Lazarus captive, freed him and a fig tree was told to die by the Lord and it did so from the root. When Joshua needed more daylight while in the heat of a battle, the sun was commanded to stand still for an hour. A rock was made into a water source by the hand of God. Moses heard the Master's voice and struck the stone out of obedience, which released the rock to bring forth.

The list is never ending and if you take a moment to reflect, there may be instances you can recall when 'something' told you. When you obey, that is when you have moved from listening to hearing. The light bulb comes on. It is a place beyond reasoning or rationalizing.

There is a stirring within you. It may not make sense to anyone but you. Hearing moves you beyond passivity into action.

"Verily, verily, I say unto you, He that heareth my word, and believeth on him that sent me, hath everlasting life, and shall not come into condemnation; but is passed from death unto life. Verily, verily, I say unto you, The hour is coming, and now is, when the dead shall hear the voice of the Son of God: and they that hear shall live."[26] John 5:24-25 KJV

---

[26] *Holy Bible KJV*: Thomas Nelson Publishers, 1984.

Chapter VI: Hand Out

When you look at the hand, what do you see? There are five digits, four fingers and a thumb. The purpose of the hand is to hold, lift, grasps, and do so many other things that are too numerous to record. One has to wonder if this appendage was not divinely orchestrated. How did evolution manage to purposely and specifically design the hand so perfectly for the many tasks they perform?

There are uses for the hand which may not come to mind readily but play a significant role in your life daily. For instance, think for a moment how often in the course of the day, your hands are used to communicate. We wave to others, shake hands, applaud, thumbs up, thumbs down, shoot the bird, point, hitchhike, etc. Every gesture described signifies an act of communication that most humans are familiar with.
Helen Keller's efforts were instrumental for starting a line of communication in the deaf and blind community. The entire body is often used to send signals and messages via body language. However, with sign language the hands play the most integral part of the conversation.

The hands have creative ability to emulate or imitate anything put before them. The levels of creativity are endless. Man's ability to design, build, erect, construct, write, compose, sew, bake, or whatever, begins with the thought but is completed by the hands. Dating back thousands of years ago, the handiwork of man's hands remained visible for all to see. Take a look at some of the creative power of man; pyramids, Mt. Rushmore, The Eifel Tower, The Sphinx, spaceships, aircrafts; fine arts such as The Mona Lisa, Beethoven's Concerts, written and played by hand. Just a quick glance at man is an indication that there is a creative power greater than himself, which is responsible for man' s origin. Can you imagine a group of ants erecting an apartment complex or primates building their own spacecraft? Yes, they have been trained to fly in them, but who builds them?

The mysteries of God are endless, and man has been given part of His greatness. All through the scriptures the hands of man are referenced and linked with power. Samson used his hands to destroy a coliseum full of his enemies by pushing down the columns. David was able to fling a rock with so much force that it brought down the mighty giant, Goliath. The hands of Noah built an ark great enough, large enough and strong enough to house the animals of the world to keep and maintain life during the great flood.

Peter and John were on the way to the temple to pray as they always did and noticed a lame beggar, who had been lame since birth outside the temple. Peter and John were not superheroes with magical powers. They had faith in God. Notice what happened:

"And Peter, fastening his eyes upon him with John, said, Look on us. And he gave heed unto them expecting to receive something of them. Then Peter said, Silver and gold have I none; but such as I have give I thee: In the name of Jesus Christ of Nazareth rise up and walk. And took him by the right hand, and lifted him up: and immediately his feet and ancle bones recovered strength."[27] Acts 3:4-7 KJV

Nothing happened until Peter took him by his right hand. God says that He will have the sheep (His people) on the right hand and the goats (the devil's people) on the left hand. The right hand signifies power. Jesus says He sits at His Father's right hand. Here is where the problem arises:

"Thy hands have made me and fashioned me: give me understanding, that I may learn thy commandments."[28] Psalm 119:73 KJV.

Sometimes the brain will misconvey information when outside influences come into play. The power is present

---

[27] *Holy Bible KJV*: Thomas Nelson Publishers, 1984.

[28] *Holy Bible KJV*: Thomas Nelson Publishers, 1984.

when it is connected to the power source. Peter spoke in the name of Jesus Christ of Nazareth and the power was released when he stretched his hand forth. What Psalm 119:73 is saying, is to have an understanding first before you move forward and make certain that you are in right standing with the power.

David was having problems with his enemies. They were triumphant over him, and he called on God. Well of course, God rescued him, but this may be the reason why:

"The Lord rewarded me according to my righteousness; according to the cleanness of my hands hath he recompensed me."[29] Psalm 18:20 KJV

Perhaps you are trying to do great things with your hands; healing, creating, building, and helping, but it just doesn't seem to work out. Maybe there has been a disconnection from the power source or there could be dirt present somewhere.

---

[29] *Holy Bible KJV*: Thomas Nelson Publishers, 1984.

Chapter VIII: Foot Notes

As this writing grows swiftly to an end, it would be befitting to finish at the end. What does this mean? Since it began at the top it just makes sense to finish at the bottom. A few years ago, Disney released a movie called ' Happy Feet'. The intent of this chapter is to help you see your feet in a new light. Looking down at your feet at this time may or may not create a smile on your face. However, what the Bible and Jesus say about your feet may change your whole outlook. Most people do not look at the bunions, corns, and ingrown toenails and receive an epiphany from God. Perhaps if you take a moment to realize how important your feet are, it's possible.

According to scripture there are several ways that the feet are referenced and reverenced. First and foremost, as previously mentioned, the feet are used as the base for the body. They have a unique design unlike most mammals. Several mammals have phalanges (fingers and toes). The primates' closet resembles man. Yet, if man evolved from apes, he acquired an extra toe along the way. Apes and monkeys do have five digits on their hands but only four toes according to the experts.[30]

---

[30] Hennessy, Kathryn et al., *Natural History*: D.K. Publishing, 2010,

The feet of man are not solely designed for climbing trees subduing enemies or securing prey; which is not to say that it is not impossible. Perhaps, the feet are shaped and fashioned for a divine purpose. Maybe that is why there are five toes because the number five represents grace.

There are several ways that the feet are referenced in the Word. However, for the sake of brevity, this writing will only address seven ways that the feet are substantial:

Transportation

Everyone who has the ability to bear weight also has the ability to move from one place to another. In Jesus' day the Bible alludes to the premise that most of His travels were via foot. In order for you to move from one place to the other, your mobility is largely dependent upon your feet. What is so miraculous about that? Well, when Jesus and Peter were walking on the water in Matthew 14:26-29 KJV. (Paraphrased) They were without jet skis. No physical change was noted in their feet, yet they could stand on water. The problem came when Peter's faith failed. Then there's the account of Elijah giving King Ahab the news that it was going to rain in I Kings 8:41-45 KJV (Paraphrased), and to hurry and get to Jezreel before the

---

534-549.

storm began. Then suddenly the Lord touched Elijah and his feet ran 20 miles. He passed the King's horse and chariot to arrive at Jezreel first.

Ownership

God told His people after leaving Egypt, that He would give them a land that flowed with milk and honey. All they had to do was possess the land. In their own eyes they saw themselves as grasshoppers before the giants, so they were afraid to go over and take the promise land. When God says it is yours, it is Yes and Amen. However, that does not mean it will just fall into your lap. Something has to be done to move your faith into receiving mode. If your faith does not become activated, then on what premise can God release that blessing? We should learn from the Israelites. They wandered aimlessly around in the wilderness for forty years, without faith in God, without trusting His Word, without the blessed assurance in Him and died.

Joshua was one of the original two who believed they could have taken the land, which they already owned because of God's promise. So when the Master spoke to Joshua:

"Every place the sole of your foot shall tread upon, that have I given unto you, as I said unto you, as I said unto

Moses."[31] Joshua 1:3 KJV.

Joshua had faith in God that He would do whatever He said He would do. For this reason, Joshua was a mighty man of God and a mighty warrior. He trusted God in all things, so he prayed before he rose up against his enemies. His victories were many - Not to mention the city of Jericho; which had an impenetrable wall, which came tumbling down, after merely marching around it for seven days.

Direction

Though your brain is in control of downloading the information, it is your feet that leads and guides you to the destination. God says it this way, *"The steps of a good man are ordered by the Lord and he delighteth in his ways."*[32] Psalm 37:23 KJV. When your will aligns with God's then He will make your feet like hind's feet, which are sure footed, confident and unwavering. Jesus tells the disciples to take up their cross and follow Him. He challenged their belief system. Can you walk away? Will you let go or give up what makes sense for what you don't yet understand? This is where all the previously stated systems come together. We are one body with many

---

[31] *The Comparative Study Parallel Bible*: Zondervan Corp, 1984.

[32] *The Comparative Study Parallel Bible*: Zondervan Corp, 1984.

members. The brain received information from a perfect stranger. The eyes see a plain ordinary man. The ears were listening but heard what He said. The words penetrated their hearts. They obeyed: the business owner, the wicked tax collector, John's disciples who were looking for more and the unbelievers. Immediately, the hands released what the world deemed as precious, and their feet followed.

Humility and Respect

These two have to come together, because without respect you will not be humble. In scripture it is noted when the men of God were encountered by an angel, they always bowed themselves to the ground at their feet. It may have been in fear as well as respect. The scriptures are too numerous to list but these three encounters are significant. The first to consider is that John the Baptist stated that he was not worthy to unlatch Jesus' sandals, let alone touch His feet. Then there is the young lady with the alabaster box who anointed the feet of Jesus in preparation of His burial. Then she dried His feet with her hair. Yet, the greatest of these, is when Jesus says:

"If then your Lord and Master have washed your feet; ye also ought to wash one another's feet. For I have given you an example, that ye should do as I have done to you."[33] John 13:14-15 KJV.

Humility is the key to holiness. As Jesus humbled Himself, as Christians, we should do likewise.

However, it is a difficult task without a relationship with the Master. Knowing that God loves you so much that He was willing to die, should evoke respect. This is what makes man God's greatest miracle: to be connected with an All mighty, All powerful, All knowing God.

Weapon

Feet being considered as a weapon of warfare may not make sense. However, when the Bible refers to tread and trample that is a direct reference to the feet. According to Webster, the word "tread" is a verb which means to press or beat with the feet.[34] In the passage of Scripture from Luke 10:19, Jesus declares, that man would be empowered to tread over serpents and scorpions and all the power of the enemy without harm. It may sound insignificant or unimportant because when stampedes occur, other animals can trample their enemies as well.

---

[33] *The Comparative Study Parallel Bible*: Zondervan Corp, 1984.

[34][34] Agnes, Michael., ed. *Webster New Dictionary and Thesaurus*: Wiley Publishing Inc,2002, 672.

Upon further examination of the above scripture, note that man was endued with this ability from God and no enemy will be able to subdue him in this matter. Perhaps, this is why it is said to keep the devil under your feet. When the devil is under your feet, it keeps him under the lowest part of your body and he must succumb to the weight thereof.

Endurance

When thinking of endurance, just being still comes to mind. In the case of the first Psalm, it says 'like a tree planted by the river (where there is a constant flow of water, which is life giving and sustaining). I shall not be moved. (Paraphrased) There is an indication that being still is powerful. Things change in the environment daily and man, though miraculous, has a tendency to waiver. When the created depends on the Creator it brings consistency and stability. The Bible declares over and over, the Importance of being still. You ask what does that have to do with your feet? Paraphrasing what Jesus said, God will fight your battles if you stand still. Stand still and know that I am God. Having done all to stand, just stand.

Kneeling is an act of submission as we kneel to pray. It is a humbling experience. Bowing signifies a gesture of total surrender as when the people encountered angels, they bowed at their feet. When you totally surrender, you acknowledge defeat. Nevertheless, it is virtually impossible to engage in combat or withstand the pressures of life lest you stand. The confidence is in standing. The strength is in the standing. The victory is in the standing. There are times in our lives that standing is all we have. We feel helpless, doubtful and oppressed.

Therefore, with God's help we are able to stand the test of time with a hope and an assurance that he is the firm foundation beneath our feet.

Power and Authority

"Behold, I give unto you power to tread on serpents and scorpions, and over all the power of the enemy; and nothing shall by any means hurt you."[35] Luke 10:19 KJV.

God makes it perfectly clear, that man has all power over the enemy. When Jesus sent His disciples out, they were told if you are accepted with gladness into a man's home, bless it, but if not shake the dust from your feet when you leave. It was not given to shake the dust from your hands or clothing. Why? Could it be that the feet would be the means by which they would enter another's home and may possibly taint that home with the residue? When God dresses His servants in preparation for spiritual

---

[35] *Holy Bible KJV*: Thomas Nelson Publishers, 1984.

battle, this is what was said about the feet; *"And having shod your feet in preparation [to face the enemy with the firm footed stability, the promptness and the readiness produced by the good news] of the Gospel of peace."* Ephesians 6:15 Amplified. Is this why the washing of feet came about? The feet travel not just the dusty roads, but in diverse and corruptible places and needed a frequent cleansing as well as peace to follow the path of God. It is implied, but not specified in the Holy Scriptures. The next time you look at your feet and ponder these questions, remember these words..." And how shall they preach, except they be sent? As it is written, *"How beautiful are the feet of them that preach the gospel of peace, and bring glad tidings of good things!"*[36] Romans 10:15 KJV.

---

[36] *The Comparative Study Bible*: Zondervan, 1984.

Conclusion

What is a miracle? Webster defines a miracle in these words: *1) An event or action that apparently contradicts known scientific laws, 2) A remarkable thing.*[37] The next time you look in the mirror focus on what you are seeing but see not. Make a note of having ears that hear not.

For sure, man fits the bill. Bishop T.D Jakes said, *"Miracles' are created out of need." Potter's House, the Famine Is Over.* Abundant Supply Series. So, who needed man? God said, *"Let us make mankind in Our own image, after Our likeness; and let them have complete authority over the fish of the sea, the birds of the air, the [tame] beasts, and over all of the earth and over everything that creeps upon the earth."*[38] Genesis 2:26 Amplified.

It appears that man was created by a power far greater than his own for a position no other living thing on Earth could handle. Perhaps, this is what virtually makes it impossible to explain man. The term human being is truly befitting because of the ability and propensity to be in

---

[37] Agnes, Michael., ed. *Webster New Dictionary and Thesaurus*: Wiley Publishing Inc., 2002, 405.

[38] *The Comparative Study Bible*: Zondervan, 1984.

constant change and adaptation mode. God's greatest miracle is always in a state of being. Mankind will never reach his fullest potential. He can always learn more, attain more, climb higher, accomplish greater, change history, make history, teach others, overcome, conquer and the list goes on endlessly.

The first few chapters in the book of Genesis give a day-by-day account of how the Earth and everything in it came to be. For a questioning mind, one might ask, what is the big deal about man? Therein, lies the passion for this writing, *"And the Lord God formed man of the dust of the ground, and breathed into his nostrils the breath of life; and man became a living soul."*[39] Genesis 2:7 KJV.

The quest to know more lies within you. Maybe you were not moved at what your eyes have seen or your ears have heard. Whether a believer or non-believer is irrelevant.

Regardless of your theory or ideology on the origin of man, the fact is you are here. Fearfully and wonderfully made are you. Gifted, powerful and unlike any other living creature on this planet. Down to every minute detail, your DNA, the numbered hairs of your head, fingerprints specifically assigned, to you, which are unreplicable, makes you unique and special.

---

[39] *Holy Bible KJV*: Thomas Nelson Publishers, 1984.

One body with many members fitly joined together for the purpose of ruling and reigning over the Earth and everything in it could only be fashioned by an Almighty, omniscient, omnipotent God. You are the essence and handiwork of His love. You are and will always be man...God's greatest miracle!

Bibliography

Agnes, Michael, ed. *Webster 'New Dictionary and Thesaurus*. Cleveland, Ohio: Wiley Publishing Inc., 2002

Bergiglio, Jorge and Skorka, Abraham. *On Heaven and Earth*. New York, New York: Image, 2015

Carlton, Richard and Shield, Benjamin., eds. *Handbook for the Soul*. Canada: Little Brown and Company, 1995

Colbert MD, Don and Colbert, Mary. *The Seven Pillars of Health*. Lake Mary, Florida: Siloam, 2007

Eadie, Betty J., *The Awakening Heart: My Continuing Journey to Love*. New York, New York: Pocket Book, 1996

Foster, Richard J., and Beebe, Gayle D., *Longing for God*. Downer's Grove, Illinois: Inter Varsity Press, 2009

Hennessy, Kathryn et al., *Natural History: The Ultimate Visual Guide to Everything on Earth*. New York, New York: D.K Publishing, 2010

McHenry, Robert, Charles Darwin. *The Origin of Species by Means of Natural Selection: The Descent of Man and Selection in Revelation to Sex*. Chicago, Illinois: Encyclopedia Britannica, Inc., 1952

Meyers, Joyce. *Battlefield of the Mind: Winning the Battle of Your Mind*. New York, New York: Faith Words Hatchette Book Group, 1995

Null PhD, Gary. *Reboot Your Brain*. New York, New York: Gary Null Publishing, 2013

Paschall, Jeremy. *God: The Ultimate Autobiography*. Tapsfield, MA: Salem House Publishers, 1987

Podesta, Martine., ed. *The Ultimate Medical Encyclopedia: Understanding, Preventing and Treating Medical Conditions.* Buffalo, New York: Firefly, 2010

Potter, Patricia A. and Perry, Anne Griffin. *Fundamentals of Nursing.* St. Louis, Missouri: Mosley, Inc., 2005

Vanzant, Iyanla. *One Day My Soul Just Opened Up*. New York, New York: Fireside, 1998

Wagman MD, Richard J., ed. *The New Complete Medical and Health Encyclopedia*. New York, New York: Downstate Medical Center, 2006

Walsh, David Neale. *Communion With God*. New York, New York: G.P. Putnam's Sons, 2000

White, Paula. *I Don't Get Wholeness... That's the Problem: Making Relationships Work*. Tampa, Florida: Paula White Enterprise, 2007

Holy Bible KJV. Nashville, Camden, New York: Thomas Nelson Publishers, 1984

The Comparative Study Parallel Bible Presenting N.I.V., N.A.S.B. AMP, K.J.V. Grand Rapids, MI: Zondervan Corp., 1984

Strong, James. *The Strongest Strong's Exhaustive Concordance of the Bible*. Grand Rapids, Michigan: Zondervan, 2001

About the Author

Dr. Sonoma Ann Carney-Suggs was born to Grace and Samuel Alexander in Nashville, Tennessee. Her late father was a Navy man, so she has lived in various areas of the country, but Nashville is where she has spent most of her life. She graduated from Pearl High School in 1971, shortly after giving birth to her first child, Tina Janee. She began nursing school as she worked as an LPN at St. Thomas Hospital and Clover Bottom Developmental Center. She had a second child, Robert Lee. She graduated from Tennessee State University with an Associate Degree in Nursing in 1989. Dr. Suggs served as a nurse for the State of Tennessee for over 30 years before retiring and moving to Lebanon, Tennessee. She is the recipient of a master's degrees in divinity and holds two Philosophical Doctorates in Christian Education and Divinity from Emmanuel Bible College. Dr. Suggs is the author of one book entitled "You Don't Know Me"—an autobiography about the tests and trials of her life and how she overcame them by the Grace of God. Her doctoral thesis has been published in the United States and is used as a teaching manuscript in several countries in Africa. In her spare time, Dr. Suggs is also a poet and she has written hundreds of poems that she is in the process of trademarking and publishing. She is the loving grandmother of seven grandchildren: Angelique, Dominique, Monique, Malique, Teyler, Gavin and Caiden.

Dr. Suggs is an ordained minister, an Evangelist, preacher, teacher, and an intercessor. She served for several years at St. Teresa Holiness Science Church in Nashville, Tennessee under the leadership of the Late. Rev. Dr. Jennie Benson Vaughn. She now serves at the Heaven's View Baptist Church under the leadership of Bishop Belita McMurry-Fite, where she is a faithful member and servant of the Lord. Dr. Suggs is a thinker whose hermeneutical and exegetical interpretation of the Bible is unique and life changing. Dr. Suggs does not take her role in ministry lightly and works daily to maintain her relationship with God so that she may lead lost souls to Christ. She desires to be a force to be reckoned with in and for the Body of Christ!

Made in USA - Kendallville, IN
80587_9780981755120
05.10.2022 1444